The Age of Dinosaurs

Meet Ankylosaurus

Written by Mark Cunningham
Illustrations by Leonello Calvetti and Luca Massini

Cavendish Square

New York

Published in 2015 by Cavendish Square Publishing, LLC
243 5th Avenue, Suite 136, New York, NY 10016

Copyright © 2015 by Cavendish Square Publishing, LLC

First Edition

Website: cavendishsq.com

This publication represents the opinions and views of the author based on his or her personal experience, knowledge, and research. The information in this book serves as a general guide only. The author and publisher have used their best efforts in preparing this book and disclaim liability rising directly or indirectly from the use and application of this book.

CPSIA Compliance Information: Batch #WS14CSQ

All websites were available and accurate when this book was sent to press.

Library of Congress Cataloging-in-Publication Data

Cunningham, Mark, 1969 - author.
Meet Ankylosaurus / Mark Cunningham.
pages cm. — (The age of dinosaurs)
Includes bibliographical references and index.
ISBN 978-1-62712-785-1 (hardcover) ISBN 978-1-62712-786-8 (paperback) ISBN 978-1-62712-787-5 (ebook)
1. Ankylosaurus—Juvenile literature. I. Title.

QE862.O65C86 2015
567.915—dc23

2014001522

Editorial Director: Dean Miller
Copy Editor: Cynthia Roby
Art Director: Jeffrey Talbot
Designer: Douglas Brooks
Photo Researcher: J8 Media
Production Manager: Jennifer Ryder-Talbot
Production Editor: David McNamara
Illustrations by Leonello Calvetti and Luca Massini

The photographs in this book are used by permission and through the courtesy of:
Dolce Vita/Shutterstock.com, 8; Anky-man/File:Lance FM.jpg/Wikimedia Commons, 8;
Jeffery M. Frank/Shutterstock.com, 8; Aurelie1/iStock/Thinkstock, 8; © SZ Photo/Scherl/The Image Works, 20;
Domser/File:Schwanzkeule von Ankylosaurus.JPG/Wikimedia Commons, 21;
Ghedoghedo/File:Ankylosaurus magniventris.jpg/Wikimedia Commons, 21.

Printed in the United States of America

CONTENTS

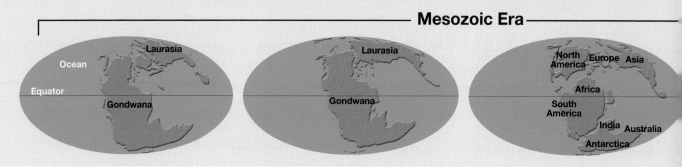

Late Triassic	Early Jurassic	Middle Jurassic
206 – 227 million years ago.	206 –176 million years ago.	176 – 159 million years ago.

A CHANGING WORLD

Earth's long history began 4.6 billion years ago. The history of our planet is divided into geological time, which includes eras, periods, epochs and ages. Among the most interesting time in Earth's past was the Mesozoic Era, which was when the dinosaurs ruled.

Dinosaur is a word that is a combination of two Greek words, *deinos* and *sauros*. Those words together mean "fearfully great lizards." These lizards lived in a world different from our own. The continents were not the same, the climate was warmer, and plant life was different—there was no grass.

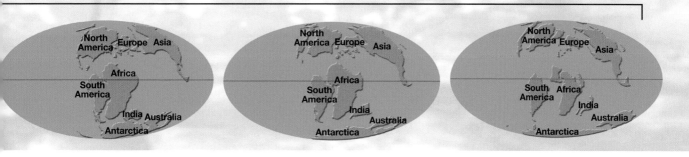

| Late Jurassic | Early Cretaceous | Late Cretaceous |
| 159 – 144 million years ago. | 144 – 99 million years ago. | 99 – 65 million years ago. |

The Mesozoic Era consists of three periods: The Triassic lasted 42 million years; the Jurassic, 61 million years; and the Cretaceous, 79 million years. Dinosaurs dominated the world for over 160 million years but became extinct nearly 65 million years before man showed up on Earth.

AN ARMORED GIANT

A member of the *Ankylosauridae* family, Ankylosaurus (pronounced ANK-ill-oh-SORE-us) belongs to the order *Ornithischia* and the infraorder *Ankylosauria*. These orders lived between the Middle Jurassic and the Late Cretaceous periods, from 162 to 65.5 million years ago.

The name Ankylosaurus comes from the Greek, meaning "lizard with fused bones." They are known as "armored dinosaurs" because their body was covered with bony plates and spines. This tough armor covered their heads, necks, backs, and heavy, clubbed tails. It was nearly impossible to break through and was used mostly for self-defense.

Ankylosaurus, an herbivorous (plant-eating) dinosaur, roamed North America from the end of the Late Cretaceous period up to about 67 to 65.5 million years ago. That was the time that the great dinosaurs became extinct. Its habitat was the coastal plain

that stretched out east of the Rocky Mountains along the western shores of a sea that crossed the interior of the continent from north to south.

Ankylosaurus was quadruped, meaning it was used to moving on all four limbs. Its body grew to measure about 11 feet (3.4 meters) in height and 22 feet (6.7 m) in length. The adult Ankylosaurus weighed as much as 13,000 pounds (5,897 kilograms).

FINDING ANKYLOSAURUS

Ankylosaurus roamed about the western United States and Alberta, Canada, from the end of the Late Cretaceous period up to about 65.5 million years ago. Ankylosaurus footprints have been found as far south as Sucre, Bolivia, in South America. The dinosaur was able to locate more than enough food in these areas as well as ward off several of its predators. That is why paleontologists believe Ankylosaurus was among the last dinosaurs to face extinction.

Scollard Formation, Alberta, Canada

Lance Formation, Wyoming

Makoshika State Park, Montana

Sucre, Bolivia

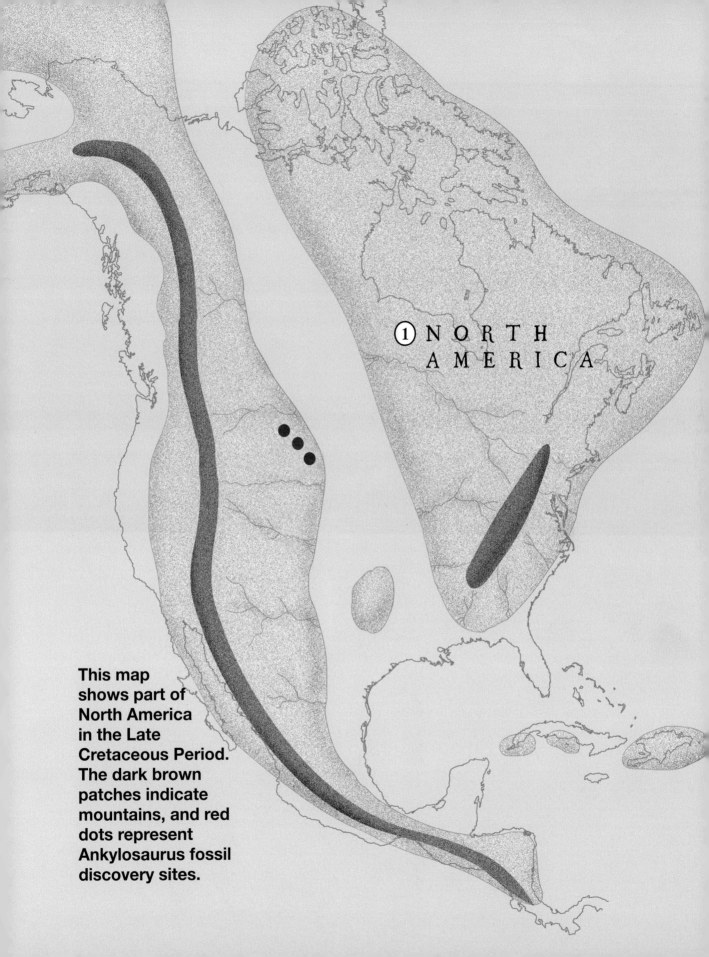

① N O R T H
A M E R I C A

This map
shows part of
North America
in the Late
Cretaceous Period.
The dark brown
patches indicate
mountains, and red
dots represent
Ankylosaurus fossil
discovery sites.

BUDDING ARMOR

Although no specimens of baby Ankylosaurs have been unearthed, paleontologists believe that their bodies were not covered with the same protective armor as their parents. This means that the baby dinosaurs would have been vulnerable to predators. Because of this, they may have stayed in groups that were surrounded by the adult dinosaurs for protection. Baby Ankylosaurus' most common predator was Tyrannosaurus Rex.

No Ankylosaurus nests, eggs, or embryos (the stage before they hatched) have been uncovered.

TEAR AND CHOP

Paleontologists believe that Ankylosaurus was an herbivorous dinosaur. The dinosaur had about 35 teeth, which it used for chopping small leaves, branches, and fruits. The front part of its snout had no teeth. Instead, it was covered with a horny beak used to tear the food from the trees.

Ankylosaurus had a keen sense of smell. This helped the dinosaur to seek out food quickly as well as avoid predators.

FRIENDLY COMPANY

Ankylosaurs roamed and lived in the same areas on Earth as the last of the horned dinosaurs. These included the large Triceratops, Hadrosaurs, and Edmontosaurus. These dinosaurs were all herbivores. Paleontologists believe that they gathered in groups to drink at the edges of the lakes scattered over the coastal plain along the inner sea of North America. The heat and humidity allowed various forms of plant life to flourish. This meant that Ankylosaurs, along with other dinosaurs, could find ample food.

HITTING BACK

Ankylosaurus had a large and bony club-like tail that was used in self-defense against predators. Its most common predator at that time was Tyrannosaurus Rex.

Ankylosaurus was a slow-moving dinosaur. Because of its heavy body and closeness to the ground, its top speed was about 6 miles (9.7 kilometers) per hour. But the bony plates covering the dinosaur's body and its armored head made up for its lack of speed. Ankylosaurus could swing its powerful tail from side to side and hurt its attacker badly, thereby driving it away.

INSIDE ANKYLOSAURUS

Ankylosaurus had a large and wide triangular-shaped head covered completely with thick bone plates. The dinosaur also had two pairs of horns attached to its skull. The club on its tail was formed by two large bony lobes—each on either side of the vertebral column. The dinosaur's body was protected by keeled scutes—or large bony projections. These scutes appear broad and large on the dinosaur's back and neck, and smaller and cone-shaped along the tail.

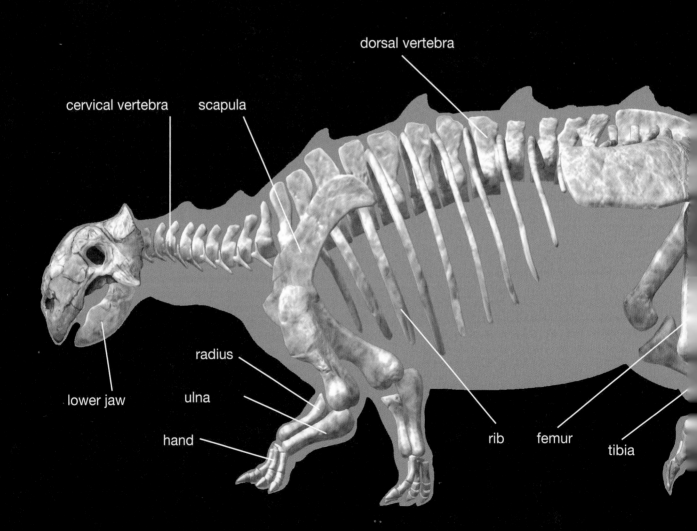

dorsal vertebra

cervical vertebra   scapula

radius

lower jaw   ulna

hand

rib   femur

tibia

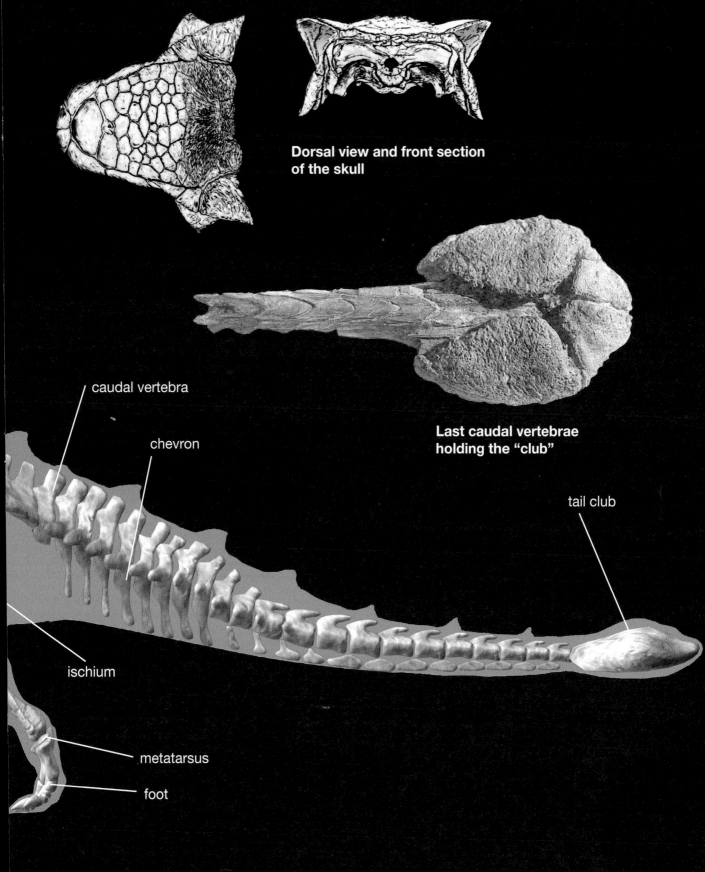

**Dorsal view and front section
of the skull**

**Last caudal vertebrae
holding the "club"**

caudal vertebra

chevron

tail club

ischium

metatarsus

foot

UNEARTHING ANKYLOSAURUS

The first Ankylosaurus fossil was unearthed in the Hell Creek Formation of Montana in 1906. A team of fossil hunters led by American paleontologist Barnum Brown discovered the dinosaur's remains. These remains included the top of a skull, sections of vertebrae, ribs, part of a shoulder, and bits of fossilized armor. Other remains were later uncovered in the Lance Formation in Wyoming and the Scollard Formation in Alberta, Canada.

No complete Ankylosaurus skeleton has ever been unearthed.

Paleontologist Barnum Brown led the team that first discovered Ankylosaurus fossils.

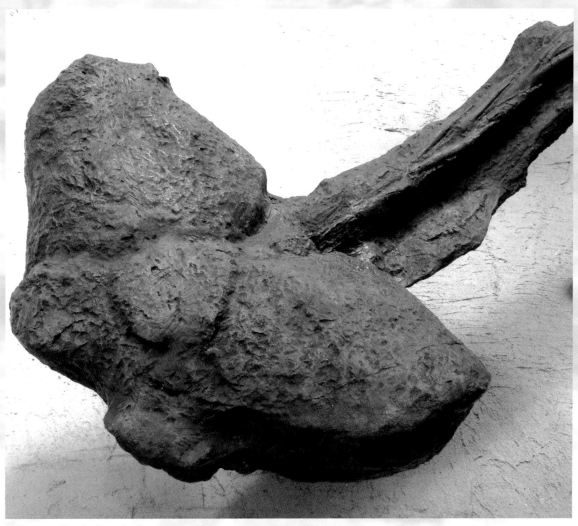

The tail club of an Ankylosaurus.

A fossil of an Ankylosaurus skull.

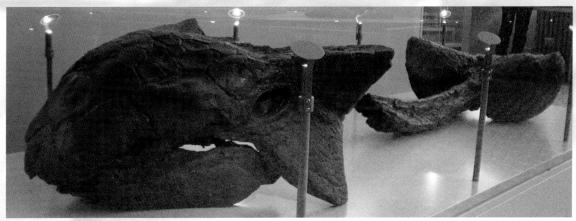

THE ANKYLOSAURIDAE FAMILY

Discovery sites of the armored dinosaurs are shown on these pages.

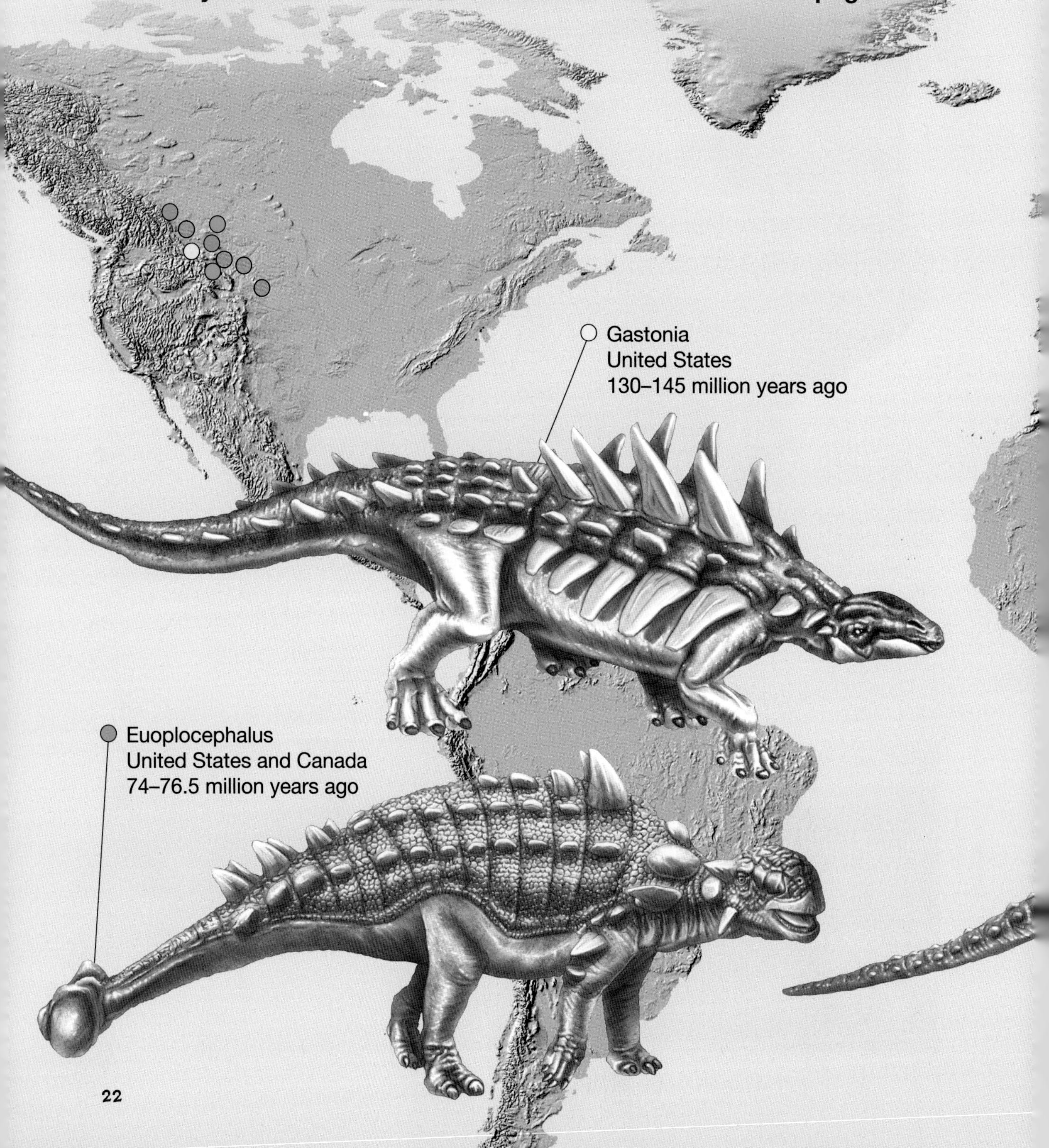

Gastonia
United States
130–145 million years ago

Euoplocephalus
United States and Canada
74–76.5 million years ago

Ankylosaurus
United States
and Canada
65.5–67 million years ago

Pinacosaurus
Mongolia and China
70–80 million years ago

Sauropelta
United States
91–116 million years ago

THE GREAT EXTINCTION

Along the Mexican coast, scientists have discovered a wide crater caused by a meteorite 65 million years ago. Based on scientific evidence, they believe that it was this meteorite that caused the dinosaurs to become extinct. The sun's rays would have been obscured by the dust suspended in the air from the impact. Without sunlight, the temperature on Earth would drop, killing many plants.

Many dinosaurs might have frozen to death due to the drop in temperature, or starved to death when the plants died and their food supplies dwindled as a result. Despite this, some scientists believe that dinosaurs did not completely die out. They feel that today's chickens and other birds are, in fact, descendants of the dinosaurs.

A DINOSAUR'S FAMILY TREE

The oldest dinosaur fossils are 220–225 million years old and have been found all over the world.

Dinosaurs are divided into two groups. Saurischians are similar to reptiles, with the pubic bone directed forward, while the Ornithischians are like birds, with the pubic bone directed backward.

Saurischians are subdivided in two main groups: Sauropodomorphs, to which quadrupeds and vegetarians belong; and Theropods, which include bipeds and predators.

Ornithischians are subdivided into three large groups: Thyreophorans, which include the quadrupeds Stegosaurians and Ankylosaurians; Ornithopods; and Marginocephalians, which are subdivided into the bipedal Pachycephalosaurians and the mainly quadrupedal Ceratopsians.

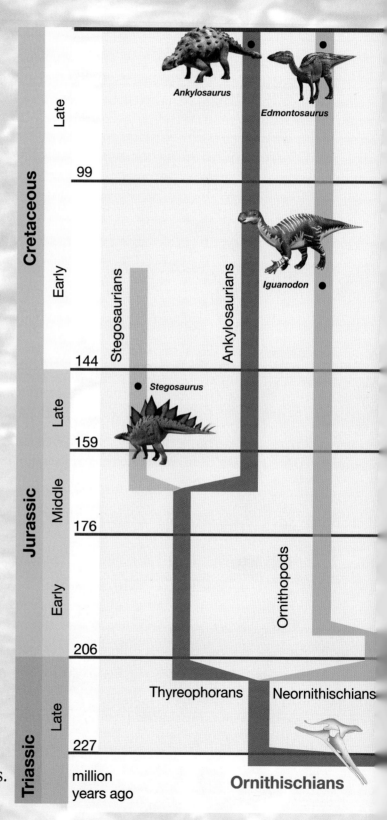

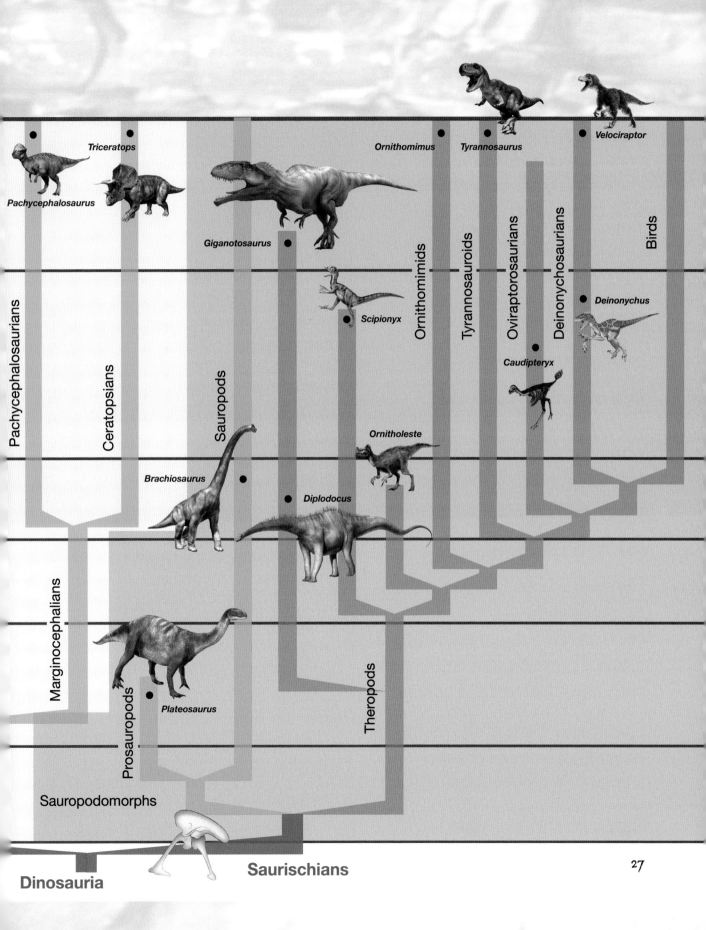

Triceratops

Pachycephalosaurus

Ornithomimus

Tyrannosaurus

Velociraptor

Giganotosaurus

Pachycephalosaurians

Ceratopsians

Ornithomimids

Tyrannosauroids

Oviraptorosaurians

Deinonychosaurians

Birds

Scipionyx

Deinonychus

Caudipteryx

Sauropods

Ornitholeste

Brachiosaurus

Diplodocus

Marginocephalians

Prosauropods

Plateosaurus

Theropods

Sauropodomorphs

Dinosauria

Saurischians

27

A SHORT VOCABULARY OF DINOSAURS

Bipedal: pertaining to an animal moving on two feet alone, almost always those of the hind legs.

Bone: hard tissue made mainly of calcium phosphate; single element of the skeleton.

Carnivore: a meat-eating animal.

Caudal: pertaining to the tail.

Cenozoic Era (Caenozoic, Tertiary Era): the interval of geological time between 65 million years ago and present day.

Cervical: pertaining to the neck.

Claws: the fingers and toes of predator animals end with pointed and sharp nails, called claws. Those of plant-eaters end with blunt nails, called hooves.

Cretaceous Period: the interval of geological time between 144 and 65 million years ago.

Egg: a large cell enclosed in a porous shell produced by reptiles and birds to reproduce themselves.

Epoch: a memorable date or event.

Evolution: changes in the character states of organisms, species, and higher ranks through time.

Extinct: when something, such as a species of animal, is no longer existing.

Feathers: outgrowth of the skin of birds and some dinosaurs, used in flight and in providing insulation and protection for the body. They evolved from reptilian scales.

Forage: to wander in search of food.

Fossil: evidence of life in the past. Not only bones, but footprints and trails made by animals, as well as dung, eggs or plant resin, when fossilized, are fossils.

Herbivore: a plant-eating animal.

Jurassic Period: the interval of geological time between 206 and 144 million years ago.

Mesozoic Era (Mesozoic, Secondary Era): the interval of geological time between 248 and 65 million years ago.

Pack: a group of predator animals acting together to capture their prey.

Paleontologist: a scientist who studies and reconstructs the prehistoric life.

Paleozoic Era (Paleozoic, Primary Era): the interval of geological time between 570 and 248 million years ago.

Predator: an animal that preys on other animals for food.

Raptor (raptorial): a bird of prey, such as an eagle, hawk, falcon, or owl.

Rectrix (plural rectrices): any of the larger feathers in a bird's tail that are important in helping its flight direction.

Scavenger: an animal that eats dead animals.

Skeleton: a structure of an animal's body made of several different bones. One primary function is to protect delicate organs such as the brain, lungs, and heart.

Skin: the external, thin layer of the animal body. Skin cannot fossilize, unless it is covered by scales, feathers, or fur.

Skull: bones that protect the brain and the face.

Teeth: tough structures in the jaws used to hold, cut, and sometimes process food.

Terrestrial: living on land.

Triassic Period: the interval of geological time between 248 and 206 million years ago.

Unearth: to find something that was buried beneath the earth.

Vertebrae: the single bones of the backbone; they protect the spinal cord.

DINOSAUR WEBSITES

Dino Database

www.dinodatabase.com

Get the latest news on dinosaur research and discoveries. This site is pretty advanced, so you may need help from a teacher or parent to find what you're looking for.

Dinosaurs for Kids

www.kidsdinos.com

There's basic information about most dinosaur types, and you can play dinosaur games, vote for your favorite dinosaur, and learn about the study of dinosaurs, paleontology.

Dinosaur Train

pbskids.org/dinosaurtrain

From the PBS show *Dinosaur Train*, you can watch videos, print out pages to color, play games, and learn lots of facts about so many dinosaurs!

Discovery Channel Dinosaur Videos

discovery.com/video-topics/other/other-topics-dinosaur-videos.htm

Watch almost 100 videos about the life of dinosaurs!

The Natural History Museum

www.nhm.ac.uk/kids-only/dinosaurs

Take a quiz to see how much you know about dinosaurs—or a quiz to tell you what type of dinosaur you'd be! There's also a fun directory of dinosaurs, including some cool 3-D views of your favorites.

MUSEUMS

American Museum of Natural History, New York, NY
www.amnh.org

Carnegie Museum of Natural History, Pittsburgh, PA
www.carnegiemnh.org

Denver Museum of Nature and Science, Denver, CO
www.dmns.org

Dinosaur National Monument, Dinosaur, CO
www.nps.gov/dino

The Field Museum, Chicago, IL
fieldmuseum.org

University of California Museum of Paleontology, Berkeley, CA
www.ucmp.berkeley.edu

Museum of the Rockies, Bozeman, MT
www.museumoftherockies.org

National Museum of Natural History, Smithsonian Institution,
Washington, DC
www.mnh.si.edu

Royal Tyrrell Museum of Palaeontology, Drumheller, Canada
www.tyrrellmuseum.com

Sam Noble Museum of Natural History, Norman, OK
www.snomnh.ou.edu

Yale Peabody Museum of Natural History, New Haven, CT
peabody.yale.edu

INDEX

Page numbers in **boldface** are illustrations.